Exploring Rock Pools

Jill McDougall

Contents

Rock Pools

Look at this!
The **tide** has gone out.
It has left pools of
water in the rocks!

There are lots of interesting creatures in rock pools.
Let's see what we can find...

Sea Stars

Sea stars can be found in rock pools.
They have five spiny arms.
Their eyes are on the ends of their arms.

A sea star's feet are very sticky. This helps it to hold onto things.

Sea stars have lots of wiggly feet. These feet help them to move. Their mouth is under their body, too.

Crabs

Crabs can be found in rock pools.
They are very good at hiding.
They hide under rocks or in the sand.

Some crabs cover their shells with seaweed to help them hide. That's clever!

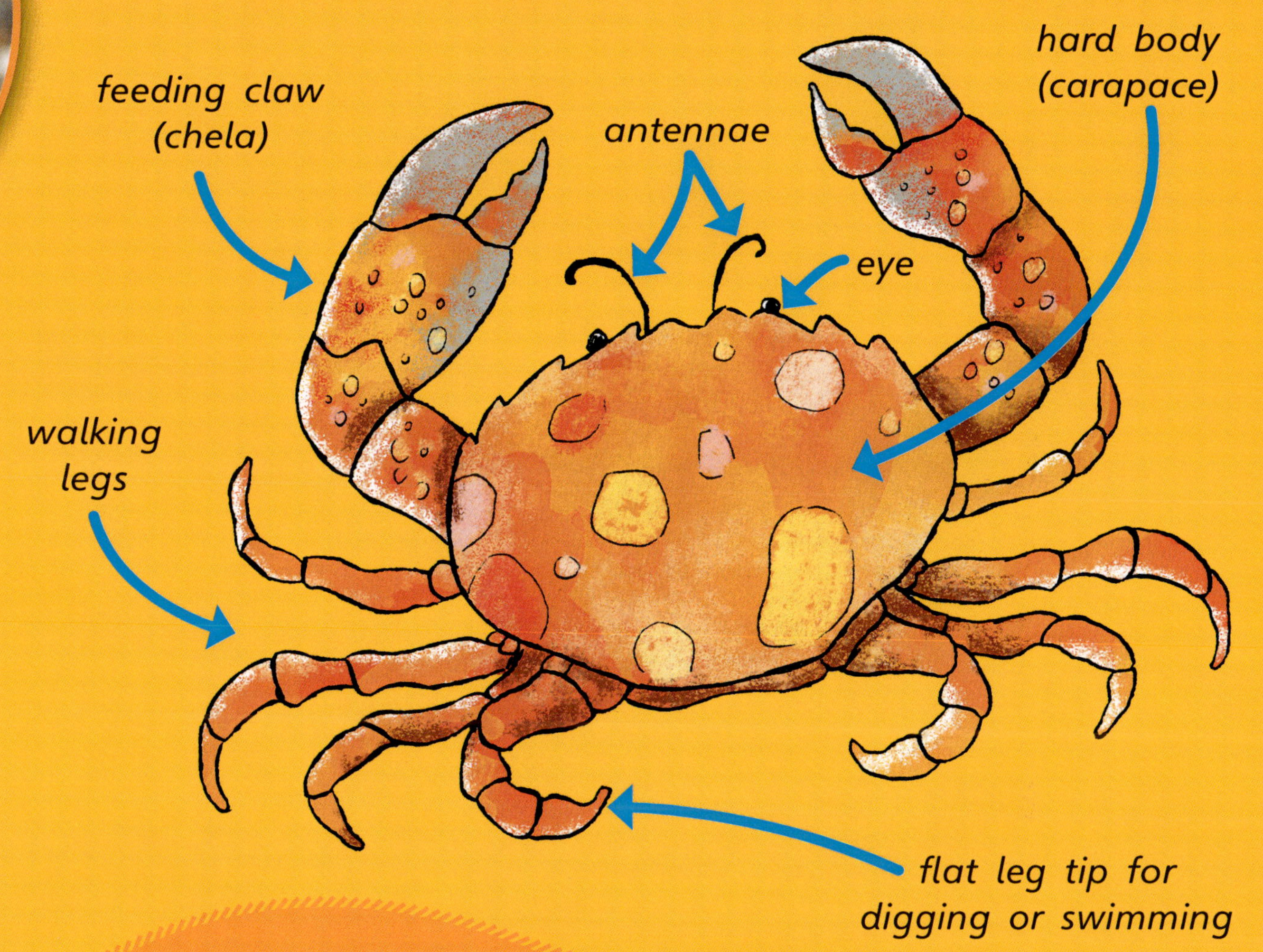

Crabs are not fussy eaters. They munch on old **seaweed** and dead fish, too.

Limpets

Limpets are a kind of sea snail.
They have a shell like a pointy hat.
Their soft body is under their shell.

Limpets eat algae. They use their shell to scrape it from rocks.

Limpets make a hole in a rock.
This hole is their home.
They leave their home to feed on **algae**.

Fish

Small fish can be found in rock pools. These fish are very fast swimmers. They dart into cracks to hide from danger.

Fish have eyes near the top of their head. This helps them to look out for danger.

Some fish can crawl on their **fins**.
These fish are called blennies.
They can even crawl to a new rock pool to find food!

What Can You See?

Look closely!

Which creatures can you see in the rock pool?

Look out!
The tide is coming in.
It's time to go!

Rock Pool Quiz

Can you guess which creatures these are?

1. I have a shell like a pointy hat.
2. I have fins.
3. I have a mouth but no head.
4. I eat dead fish.

Answers **1** limpet **2** fish **3** sea star **4** crab

Glossary

algae simple plants that have no roots or leaves

fins parts of a fish that help it move

seaweed plants that grow in saltwater

tide the movement of the seas, towards and away from the land